To

One & All

With Love & Prayers

Elizabeth [illegible]

4th J[illegible]

A Pocketful of Love

Elizabeth Trott

authorHOUSE®

AuthorHouse™ UK Ltd.
500 Avebury Boulevard
Central Milton Keynes, MK9 2BE
www.authorhouse.co.uk
Phone: 08001974150

First published by AuthorHouse 7/1/2009

ISBN: 978-1-4389-7601-3 (sc)

This book is printed on acid-free paper.

Contents

Someone's Trying My Patience

Someone's trying my patience,

Pass the shotgun - please!

Is it my imagination?

Or is someone getting at me?

At times I feel I'm being used,

By their own want – not need,

Others thinking of themselves,

Not for others sakes.

So they look good in others eyes,

Or letting their lives take.

Our opportunities are scarce today,

To others freely give.

Our lives are read by many men,

By those who think they know.

They see the outside, see the glow,

But how much do they know?

For in our hearts and lives we see,
What others cannot find.
They dread to look into themselves,
And see what they might find.
The doubt, the fear, the anger there,
It really does exist.
But far beyond, when all is seen,
They really forget to care.
They don't want to look beyond that point
To see what they have missed.
The opportunity of God's Love,
Is shining through their midst.

Oh Bother!

Oh Bother!

It's on the blink again.

This T.V. – it has to go!

The video went to be repaired,

I've heard they're on go slow.

The telephone is playing up,

In-coming only – please!

The cat is having kittens,

Thank goodness – we've got no fleas.

Her box – where has it gone?

Those kids – they've shifted it again.

Just more time, I think I need,

To find myself again.

Now – stop and Think,

And Wait again.

Now – where did I hear that Voice?

Amid the noise and busyness,

THAT ONE, STILL CALMING VOICE.

Ouch!

OUCH! What was that for?
What do you mean?
You don't like my face?
I'm not as big and ugly as you are,
But there's nothing to take it's place.
I might be small and timid,
But as chopsy as I please.
It doesn't mean that I'm afraid,
To stand and fight – if need.
You're Bullying me – you Thug!
Pick on someone your own size.
I haven't done a thing to you.
So get out of my sight.
You're big and mean, and I'm not those.
I don't like playing your games.

What you say's goes,

No room for co-operation.

A little friendship – now and then,

Really goes to show

How much a person really cares.

Their character learns how to grow.

To show their things with others,

It gives a certain glow.

They learn that giving something.

Get's something in return.

Like Friendship, Trust and Caring,

But the most they learn from this.

Is that it gives Great Joy.

Not much I know.

But to me you see,

It's One of God's Greatest Gifts.

Stressed

I'm really stressed,
I can't even think.
Anymore hassles,
I'll go over the brink!

Who needs all the aggro?
Who needs all the pain?
Is it all worth it?
No pleasure, no gain.

I can't go on,
Where will I turn?
Is it all worth it?
When will I learn?

I'm not on my own,
I've had to learn.
There's someone beside me,
Somewhere to turn.

From family to friends,
Those who are close.
I know You are there Lord,
I need not boast.

I know You are there Lord,
In all that I do.
I know that You guide me,
And help me through.

So give me Your strength Lord,
And help me in time.
Show me Your way Lord,
For You to shine.

When All Around

When all around are losing theirs,
It's important to keep your head.
When they seem to be in a panic,
You must remain fast-stead.

When all around are sinking,
And can't control a thought.
We must hold our course,
And know it's not for nought.

So when they're in a panic,
And don't know what to do.
We put our Trust in Jesus,
To us He's always True.

A Father Is

A Father is someone who loves you,
No matter what you do.
Someone you can rely on,
To you he's always true.

He loves us when we're angry,
He loves us when we're sad.
He loves us when we're happy,
And things don't seem so bad.

He's always there to comfort,
To share in all our joy.
He's also there to chide us,
When things go awry.

He gives us love so total,
We do not know its' depth.
God's love is unconditional,
Beyond our own concept.

He only asks you love Him,
And He will be your guide.
His treasures He will give you,
And is forever at your side

Not Nearly Frozen

It's not nearly frozen,
Is it you or me?
It's not nearly frozen,
Is it God's will for me?

Am I alive?
Or in deep freeze?
Do I have feelings?
Or jelly for knees?

Have I been listening?
Lord – what did You say?
Of course I've been listening
Oh boy – what a day!

I don't know what to say Lord,
It's not my domain.
If I get involved,
They'll think I'm a pain.

They'll say that I'm pushy,
Don't know what to say.
They'll say I'm a nuisance,
Get out of the way.

Excuse me – one minute,
Please can I help?
I'm willing to learn,
But I'm only a whelp.

It isn't so easy,
To listen and learn.
To have guidance from others,
I've so much to learn.

Well – okay – here goes,
I'll do what You say.
It's all in Your Hands Lord,
Just guide me I pray.

Me

Calvin Klein, Emmanuel,

Are they really me?

Versace, Armani, many more,

They're on the BBC.

Adidas, Nike, or Puma,

It's something to be seen

You've got to have some street cred,

In these I must be seen.

Sony is acceptable,

Phillips - not to bad.

An Alba isn't worth it,

Anything else is just too sad.

I've got to be in fashion,

The best of all I've seen.

You see I'm not acceptable,

If what I own – isn't of the cream.

My friends just might accept me,

My family – think I'm strange.

But God above just Loves me,

His Love covers ALL the range.

Doubt

I don't think I can do it,
Don't you mean can't?
There is no such wording,
I think I mean shan't.

I don't know how to say it,
Or even, if I should?
How would I say it?
Or even, if I could.

How do I tell them?
Is it better to show?
Do I tell boldly?
Or soften the blow?

I need to tell them rightly,
In words strong and true.
But even if I tell them,
Will clear air turn blue?

I'll pray for God's guidance,
In all that I do.
I'll ask for His strength,
And help to stay true.

So with God's blessing,
I'll do what I can.
And through His grace,
Continue with His plan.

Don't Dare To Be

I don't dare to be a Daniel,
Speaking to a king.
Or be a gentle Joseph,
Giving life, the greatest thing.

I couldn't be a Hannah,
A Ruth or even Joel.
I wouldn't even dare to,
How could I bare my soul?

I don't know how to serve Lord,
Or how to do Your will.
I don't know what to do Lord,
Or if it is Your will.

Show me what to do Lord,
And help me to be me.
Guide me in Your Way Lord,
That I should be made We.

I know We'll work together,
In everything We do.
So give me strength and guidance,
Together We'll see it through.

I Didn't Doubt

I didn't doubt to see Your face
Or what lay behind.
To see the pain and agony,
You bore for All mankind.

I also saw the Love You had,
The Life You freely gave
It wasn't just for me You came.
But, All mankind to save.

So teach me Lord,
To do Your will.
And help me Lord,
Your Word fulfil.

Help me to show the Love You have,
A guide to others be.
Help me to answer what You know,
So they might bend the knee.

Please guide me Lord, in all I do,
To show to all I know.
That Life in You has everything,
From You, I learn and grow.

So give me strength and wisdom,
And silence when in need.
But help me Lord in moments,
When for salvation sinners plead.

Strength

I've given it some thought Lord,
I need to seek Your face.
I don't think I can do it,
Without Your strength and grace.

I know I'm only human,
But ALL things can be done.
Through the grace and favour,
Of God's Only Son.

I only have to ask Lord,
I know You'll see me through.
Just give me strength and courage,
Help me to be true.

Direct me in Your paths Lord,
Guide my straying feet.
Give me grace and wisdom,
Make my life complete.

I Know

He's pushed the wrong buttons
What do I do?
He's pushed the wrong buttons
It just won't do.

I don't want to do it
I don't really care.
I really can't face it
Who really cares?

I know that he loves me
I know that he cares.
I know that I love him
The pressures not fair.

I know how to do it
And what should be done.
I don't want to face it
When all's said, and done.

I want time for freedom
To watch things go by.
To sit back and see things
And let time just fly.

I want to get off
Say goodbye to the world.
Just for a rest
Then return to this world.

I know that it's waiting,
And it must be done.
Just leave me in peace
And let me have fun.

Let me be selfish
For just one day.
Let me be only
Then back in the fray.

Just let me be freedom
And let me be – go.
Away from the pressures
Then find my way home.

DAD

I thought I'd said goodbye to you
And found I never did.
I thought I'd finally said farewell
Instead I ran and hid.

I bottled all my feelings
And held them all inside.
I pushed aside emotions
And let my life just glide.

You brought me in this world to live
To stand up straight and true.
You taught me how to laugh and cry
And see colours of every hue.

You taught me right
And showed me wrong.
That it's ok to be weak
And ok to be strong.

You showed me Faith
And where it's found.
From that of a child
To its' parent unbound.

You showed me love unfailing
Gave unconditionally;
Your time you gave unstinting
And all so willingly.

You never failed to Love us
No matter what we'd do.
You cared and showed compassion
Lifting others who felt blue.

A lifetime spent of giving
A lifetime filled with care.
A lifetime of commitment
One I was privileged to share.

When

A friendly face,
A caring smile.
Helps me to sit
And chat a while.

When to talk,
When to listen.
Give support
When tears glisten.

Encouragement here,
Advice just there.
Coffee to drink
A comfy chair.

Someone to talk to,
Someone to share.
A complete stranger
Who knows how to care.

You helped me to share
My sorrow and joy.
My thanks for tomorrow
And all they employ.

One Step

Life is very difficult,
Take one day at a time.
One foot after another,
Let your Faith just shine.

Take one day as a moment,
And savour as it comes.
Not worry for tomorrow,
Those thoughts you should shun.

Just take the day as given,
And see what God has done.
For us, there's no tomorrow,
So, see God's Glory come.

Just one foot, then another,
One step at a time.
Let God's Word just guide you,
And let His Spirit shine.

So ask the Lord for guidance,
And do His Blessed Will.
Then in the midst of silence,
His Voice will guide you still.

Mistakes

The mistakes that I've been making,
Are too many to be told.
But as I'm growing older,
In my memory they'll unfold.

The things I've said,
And shouldn't have done.
With it all over,
From my memories I run.

I shouldn't have done it
I know that it's wrong.
But just at that moment,
I felt quite strong.

I know what I'm doing,
I think that I'm right.
When it comes down to it,
I'm not very bright.

Lord, help me to listen,
Guide me I pray.
Direct my footsteps,
Where, not to stray.

So Lord, give me guidance,
Help me I Pray.
In finding true meaning,
In You are the Way.

Too Busy

So many things need doing,
No time to get them done.
The way that things are going,
I think I'll get a gun!

No time for things like standing still,
There's jobs; there to be done.
If I go slow; I'll just stop,
I'll do them on the run.

I need to be get going,
I have to do my sums.
There's lots of things need doing,
I need to get them done.

I'm going round in circles,
I'm losing it 'I wail'.
Just like a dog gone silly,
Chasing my own tail.

I need to stop and think Lord,
What do I do today?
Stop me in my tracks, Lord,
Help me listen when I pray.

Lord, show me where I'm going
And how to do Your Will.
Help me to keep on walking,
And sometimes to be still.

Money Isn't Everything

Just because you're famous,
Or just think you are.
You own a status symbol,
Yacht, plane, expensive car.

Does money buy you everything?
Bring happiness or despair?
Do people really love you?
Or do you say that 'I don't care.'

Money is not the beginning,
It isn't even the end.
It's there to make life easier
To get by and some comfort lend.

It sometimes gives us headaches,
At times it brings us joy.
There never seems enough of it,
Is it just a ploy?

But money isn't everything,
To those who know the Lord.
There's Love and Joy and Service,
And knowledge from God's Word

So even if you're famous,
Remember in God's Word,
That all in His sight are precious,
He wants to be your friend and Lord.

To Buy

Up the hill,

Down the vale.

Man has a question,

Is it for sale?

Does it have a price?

What can it be?

I really want it,

This is for me.

I don't need it

I just want.

The cost doesn't matter,

I'll be blunt.

But there's more to life,

Than buy and sell.

There's life in Heaven,

Or life in hell.

God saw man's sin,

For this He cried.

He gave us Christ Jesus,

Who for us bled and died.

So consider your future,

To buy or to sell.

Eternal life in Heaven,

Or misery in hell.

Peace and Quiet

A little peace and quiet,
That is all I ask.
Nothing so enormous,
Is it such a task?

A time to stop and listen,
To hear, what is around.
To listen to the silence,
To hear the smallest sound.

To take the time to listen,
To what God has to say.
To hear it in the silence,
Just watch and wait and pray.

So help me Lord to listen,
To what You have to say.
Teach us to be silent,
To hear Your voice each day.

Duty

I've done my duty
Everything done.
What can I do now?
Twiddle my thumbs?

My paperwork's finished,
The housework - complete.
It's time for a coffee,
To put up my feet.

The kids are all quiet,
It's time to relax.
Sit back and think,
What are the facts?

I tend to forget,
In the quiet of the day.
When into the chaos,
My thoughts tend to stray.

I just don't listen,
Or not tune in.
To what You are saying,
It gets lost in the din.

Do we listen when He tells us
Of all the things He's done?
Do we tell Him that we've heard Him
And done the things we've done?

Lord; help me to listen,
To hear what You say.
Without Your guidance,
I'm likely to stray.

So when it's quiet,
And all is at rest.
Lord, just remind me,
Not all are a pest.

Lord, help me to listen
Also to ask.
Lord help me and guide me,
It's not a task,

So when I forget Lord,
Give me a nudge.
To listen, then talk Lord,
I do have to budge.

Help me to remember,
I have work to do.
Help me to do it,
And to be true.

Do My Best

Reading, writing,
And arithmetic.
I can't do these,
I'm too thick.

My reading's bad,
My writing's worse.
My maths is useless,
Slower than a hearse.

I can see the problem,
It doesn't make sense.
All of my answers,
Are in past tense.

I'll keep on trying,
I'll do my best.
And with God's help,
Catch up with the rest.

Sayings

Patience is a virtue,

Possess it if you can.

Seldom found in woman,

Never found in man.

Be careful what you wish for,

You know, it might come true.

Be careful what you grasp for,

It could be something you may roué.

So what are in these sayings?

Could any of it be true?

And if you really doubt it,

It's God's way of teaching you.

It could be your hearts desire,

But is it good for you?

Do you want to live in God's poverty?

Or in His love, and be completely true?

Our trials are sent to try us,
Our strengths, they're sent to seek.
Our weaknesses are found out,
Our Souls to made feel weak.

Our characters are building,
On solid Love and ground.
Our weaknesses are strengthened,
By God's Love; which still surrounds.

Our tempers we lose quickly,
Our patience running out.
But God is always with us,
As everything we doubt.

The trials, He makes easier,
Our character to build.
That we might tell some other,
And say, your shoes we filled.

We might feel sad and lonely,
Set from the world apart
But God is standing with us,
Giving Love with All His Heart.

He knows how much we Love Him,
He knows how much we care.
But do we know the burden,
Or the hurts, He cannot share?

The trials that He sends us,
Are meant to help us grow.
That when it comes to others,
Its God's Grace that we then show.

We can say "That I have been there"
And "Done the things you did"
But by God's grace overcame them,
And now I wish to live.

So when you feel so lonely,
And trials seem to overcome.
Remember that you're learning,
To teach others of God's Kingdom Come.

Silence

Silence is Golden,

Enjoy it while you can.

You might be interrupted,

That's not in the plan.

We like to hear the quiet,

Nothing to distract.

Nothing to disturb you,

Until the noise is back.

But what is in the silence?

Is it the wind, or sounds of air?

Is it the sound of birds just singing?

Or the smells that fill the air?

Do we hear what's in the silence?

Do we know what's really there?

Do we listen for it's content?

Do we know that God is there?

Do we listen for God speaking?

Do we listen for His call?

Do we wait to hear His reason?

Do we hear Him when He calls?

Do we listen when He tells us?
Of all the things He's done.
Do we tell Him that we've heard Him?
And done the things we've done.

Do we tell Him that we Love Him?
Do we say I'm sorry Lord?
I forgot to hear You calling,
I was busy with my world.

So when your world is silent,
Stop, listen, look and see.
Then you will hear God saying,
I made the world for all to see.

I sent My Son to save you,
I gave Him willingly.
He gave His life to save you,
You gladly bent the knee.

When all around is noisy,
Look to the silence, not the din.
It's there that you will find Me,
Guiding you from sin.

To Others

In days of old, when knights were bold,
With damsels in distress.
No one seemed to care much,
What went on within their chest.

Confederates on your doorstep,
Yankees come to call.
It didn't seem to matter,
If for Salvation you did call.

It doesn't really matter,
Of where you live or fall.
There are those who threaten,
For Salvation you must call.

In All the world around us,
Their sin is in abound.
It is for us as Christians,
To spread God's Word around.

Does it matter who we speak to?
Does it matter what we're called?
Does it matter that God chose us?
It's for us to do our all.

We want to do God's biding,
And do His Blessed Will.
Be still and Pray; then comes the day,
My beating heart; be still.

I'll try to do Your Will Lord,
And often speak Your Name.
If not I'll show them how Lord,
Not live my life in shame.

I'll guide them to Your mercy,
Your Love and guiding Light.
But help me in my frailty,
By Your strength and might.

Tomorrow

Tomorrow never comes they say,
Is it really true?
Does the very thought of it.
Give you chills right thru'?

Does planning for tomorrow,
Or yesterday's today.
Give you vivid nightmares?
To fear – don't give way.

Just give the time to Jesus,
Let Him make the plans.
Just leave your fears and worries,
In His Loving Hands.

Don't worry for tomorrow,

Even though it comes.

You've slept all night, it's alright,

God has done His sums.

So wait upon Lord Jesus,

See what He has to say.

Then ask Him for His guidance,

While you sit and pray.

So give up all your worries,

Leave them at Jesus' feet.

Receive God's Joy and Happiness,

In His Love complete.

Listen

I'm sitting here in silence,
Waiting for Your call.
Do I have the patience?
Will I fail and fall?

Will I make the grade Lord?
Can I do Your Will?
Help me find Your Peace Lord,
Help me to be still.

Help me listen to the silence,
Hear You when You call.
Guide me when I fail Lord,
Help me to stand tall.

Help me do Your will Lord,
In everything I do.
Not for my own glory,
But all for Love of You.

A Child

I couldn't see the meaning Lord,
In what You had to say.
It seemed very jumbled,
Until the break of day.

You said 'Go out and claim them',
'And bring them to your King'.
For every one Salvation,
The heaven's break forth and sing.

A child is born in glory,
The earthly man is gone.
No one there to grieve it,
In heaven a brand new song.

A child will need its parents,

A guiding hand you see.

A task as older Christians

Is up to you and me.

So when a child is growing,

Tries to run before it walks.

You are there for guidance,

There for chats and talks.

So remember we were children,

And guided by His Hand.

Then we must do so – likewise,

And help these children stand.

Unconditional Love

Someone to hold onto,

Someone to love.

Is it just possible?

A gift from above.

No worries, or fears,

No one to place any blame.

Just someone to love me

I'm not asking for fame.

Someone to love me,

Through right or wrong.

Someone who loves me

For them I'll be strong.

As long as they love me,

For who that I am

I'll love them whatever,

And do what I can.

Could somebody love me?
With all of my faults.
Would somebody love me?
Should I hide in dark vaults?

How do I doubt
That someone may care?
When friends turn and ask me
How does life fare?

I talked to a friend,
Their face, all aglow.
Telling me of a Saviour,
That I might know.

Of how much Christ loved me,
He died on a tree.
Unconditional Love,
For a sinner; like me.

Standing

Standing there,

So strong and tall.

When chaos comes,

Will they fall?

Looking up,

To see above.

What comes down?

Unconditional Love.

A Christian's job,

When said and done.

Is to show God's Love,

And what He's done.

How He sent His Son,
Who lived and died.
Jesus Christ,
Who was crucified.

He bore our sins
To give us life.
Tho' our earthly time,
Will find some style.

But Eternity waits,
For those He calls.
For those who answer,
Heavens golden walls.

Love

Do I need to know your name?
It's engraved upon my hand.
My Love for You will never die,
It's like the endless sand.

Not shifting here from place to place,
Or moving all around.
But in the fact, it's always there,
Beneath you, like solid ground.

I'll always be there for You,
No matter what you do.
For where you are, there I'll go,
Whatever you're going through.

In good times and in bad,
Whatever you may feel.
My Love will always be there,
To tell you, that I'm real.

My Love for You will never die,
No matter what you do.
I died, that you might live with Me,
For ALL Eternity through.

I lived a Life, a sinless Life,
And knew the joys of man.
Yet, Died for you in agony,
To complete my Father's plan.

Our Love for You is so complete,
Your angers, We forgive.
We see the hurt; We see the pain,
But, Our Gift is for you to live.

I came but once, to claim My own,
To teach them how to give.
I'm coming back, to bring My Crown,
With Eternal Life, for You to live

A New Life

A new life beginning,
Two become one
A new life beginning,
Heavenly songs sung.

A new life in Jesus,
Your Friend and Lord.
A new life in Jesus,
Learn to live by His Word.

A new life in Jesus,
Don't worry or doubt.
A new life in Jesus,
Tell it about.

So tell it to others,
Shout the good news.
You've a new life in Jesus,
Give them the news.

Tell Them

The house is very quiet,
There's something missing here.
I hear it in the silence,
Is there someone there?

I hear a voice that whispers,
Listen to what I say.
I have a little job for you,
It starts for you today.

You are to take my message,
To others who might hear.
To tell them that I love them,
And tell them that I care.

So boldly go and tell them,
My love is all around.
I will not condemn them,
Though sin is all around.

Tell them that I love them,
I died upon the tree.
Defeated death rose again,
From sin to set them free.

I've gone to live in Glory,
Their places to prepare.
So tell them the Old, Old Story,
Their heavenly home is in my care.

Who Put Glitter

Who put glitter
In the sky?
A thing of beauty,
To draw the eye.

The twinkling lights,
The glowing stars.
The many planets,
Including Mars.

A handiwork,
Not seen by man.
A thing of beauty,
All of God's plan.

Man's still learning,
Of this wondrous place.
But forgets to receive,
Of God's wondrous grace.

God made it all,
His wonderful plan.
Sun, stars and moon,
Earth – right down to man.

Paintbrush

A paintbrush,
Swept across the sky.
The colours there,
Did please the eye.

In shades of blue,
With clouds of white.
The beauty there,
Was a glorious sight.

With gold's and pinks,
Of various hues.
Of the Masters Hand,
There are no clues.

To see these sights,
Man doesn't understand.
That these wondrous gifts,
Are from Gods' Hand.

God gave these gifts,
That we might share.
In a beautiful world,
Beyond compare.

A Marvellous Thing

A Child is born,
What a marvellous thing.
Spread the good news,
The angels did sing.

The heavens are alight,
With a heavenly host.
Peace, goodwill to all men,
From the Holy Ghost.

Shepherds did see Him,
They brought Him a lamb.
What a wonderful insight,
For God's Son of Man.

Incense and Gold,
To show He was King.
Myrrh, so sweet smelling,
Signified His suffering.

From birth to His death,
It was all in Gods plan.
To show to all men,
Jesus Christ – Son of Man.

Gifts

You give Peace,
Like no one else can.
All part of
Your gift to man.

You give us Faith,
A lot of Grace.
To live life full,
At today's fast pace.

You give us laughter,
You give us joy.
All of these gifts,
We, Your children employ.

To show to others,
Your great Love.
To tell them all,
Of Your home above.

So give us strength,
To others show.
For wisdom we ask,
To let others know.

Appreciate

Do we really appreciate,
The things that God has done?
He gives us golden sunshine,
To show His Work is done.

He gives us rain refreshing,
The breeze to lift the air.
He gives the roaring hurricane,
To show that He is fair.

The gentle swirl of winter,
The blizzard in it's' might.
The waking of the springtime,
Tornados in full flight.

The creatures of the wilderness,
The birds in their full flight.
The mighty ocean creatures,
Those that roam at night.

Our families He gives us,
In trouble they are there.
While others in our midst,
Try to show that they don't care.

God above just Loves us,
He sent His Son to show.
A heavenly home awaits us,
Our hearts He wants to know.

God's Greatest Gift

A tree was made into a Cross,
Upon Mount Calvary.
The Son of Man, He lived and died,
For Your Eternal Liberty.

He taught God's Word,
And showed His Love.
That in accepting Him,
We'd live in Heaven above.

His back was scourged,
His beard pulled out.
He suffered in silence,
Without a doubt.

He carried His cross,
Wore a Crown of thorns.
To those He'd shown Love,
They now poured out scorn.

They drove nails in His hands,
And into His feet.
A spear in His side,
When His death was complete.

But death had been conquered,
And so had hell.
Jesus Blood is ALL cleansing,
It makes us all well.

Acceptance of Jesus,
Into Your Heart.
As Saviour and Friend,
It's just the start.

There's newness to Life,
A fullness of Joy.
A Life that's Eternal,
With Christ to enjoy.

A Gift

A gift is a gift,
Whatever we say.
A gift is a gift,
At the end of the day.

Whoever the giver,
Whoever receives.
Whatever the present,
It's meant to please.

A gift that is greatest
Is given with Love.
A gift that was greatest,
Was sent from above.

A child that was given,

Grew into a man.

A life that was given,

All part of God's plan.

The gift that was given,

Was all of God's plan,

His Son Christ Jesus

Gods' Son of Man.

The gift that was given,

Was life in the end.

For our place in Heaven,

In eternity to spend.

Christmas Time

It's Christmas time
What does it mean?
Christ is born,
To die on a tree!

He lives a life,
Commits no sin.
The Perfect Man,
For Souls to win!

He lived a life,
In human form.
A child He was,
A baby born.

In life He grew,
Knew aches and pains.
Knew grief and loss,
Healed others pains.

Knew Love and Joy,

Peace and gain.

Knew others fears,

Gave peace again.

In all His life,

He freely gave.

His Father's Love,

And peace they craved.

He gave His All,

E'en unto death.

He loved them all,

To His latest breathe.

He died,

That we.

Might live with peace,

And others learn of Him.

He gave His Life,

That we might live.

That eternity,

Is a Gift – through Him.

The Truth Behind Christmas

The Christmas Tree is coming down,
The festive season over.
Maybe it just seems this way,
That we are getting older

The childhood fun of Christmas
The fun that came our way.
It didn't really bother us,
The truth of Christmas Day.

When God came down at Christmas,
A baby He was born.
To Mary and poor Joseph,
In a stable all forlorn.

The angels they did herald,
His birth for all to know.
The shepherds they came seeking,
Their hearts were all aglow

When just a child, bare walking,
The Wise Men, they did come.
When warned of Herod's actions,
Their promise they did shun.

The truth behind our Christmas,
No matter what men say.
Is Truth and Light, God's purest Love,
Our Saviour – Alive today.

Checklist

Cards	Check	
Presents	Check	
Kids	Check	
Packing	Check	
Coffee	Check	Not Check
Kids – At Auntie's	Check	
Car	Check	
Hotel	Check	Not Check

Me or him to check it?

Me of course, can't you see!

Good evening, can I check my reservation

24th – 26th December of course.

The deposit was paid in September

Confirmation then came through the door.

I'm sorry – you say it's been cancelled

The hotel is way overbooked.

You've sent us a letter with refund

And vouchers for us to rebook.

I know that Christmas is busy

There isn't a "Room at the Inn"

I just have trouble believing

Can I put an extra claim in?

I'll book somewhere, not far to go

Or get that Same Old Story?

Used 2 thousand years ago!

New Year

It's New Year –Yes!

What will it bring?

I've a party tonight

I need a new dress.

Old year meets New,

What will it mean?

Do I have time?

I can't stop and dream.

I'm meeting new people,

What will I say?

How nice to see you,

Did you have a good day?

They'll think, and they'll wonder,

Put it back on the shelf.

I know that I'm normal,

Don't look like an elf.

In time they'll accept me,

For who, what I am.

They'll even ask questions,

I'm not a battering ram.

I'll not fight with others,

Stay calm, cool and poised.

I'm frightened to death,

Oh boy, what a noise.

Oh well! It's all over,

I've said my piece.

A time to relax,

Within God's Given Peace.

Lightning Source UK Ltd.
Milton Keynes UK
17 June 2010

155733UK00001B/52/P